Kelly

Hope the travels go
well + keep in touch.
It has been a pleasure
working with you. I
will miss your upbeat
personality + jokes.

Kathy Jernigan   Kay
10315 Outlaw Bend
Converse, TX 78109

Feb. 9

74
So
TX. 78224

Beauty of
Texas

Elizabeth Keefer.
6901 Scottswood.
San Antonio.
TX 78239
(210) 946-0520

Kelly -
(Howdy). Really sorry you
are leaving. I've had fun listening
to you. Have fun + maybe you'll be
a movie star! Good Luck

Shirly Patterson
6935 Crestway Dr #36
San Antonio, TX 78239

Dear Kelly;
Best of luck; a rolling stone
gathers no moss but it sure collect
a lot of pictures.

Julin Rodrigues MD

Kelly;
Sure had a lot of fun with
you talking all the time. Hope
your travels go well. Hope Mr.
Right comes into your life soon!
Good luck and always remember
you have friends here! Don't forget
us. We will never forget you. Never!
Never! Never I ever! You are so special
Nurse. Don't let anyone tell you other
wise !!.

Marilyn Bentley town
12837 Fairy town
San Antonio, Texas 78233.

Beauty of
Texas

Text: Robin Will
Concept & Design: Robert D. Shangle

Revised Edition
First Printing August, 1992
Published by LTA Publishing Company
Division of Renaissance Publishing Company, Inc.
318 East 7th St., Auburn, IN 46706

"Learn about America in a beautiful way."

This book features the photography of
James Blank
Shangle Photographics
Robert Shangle

Library of Congress Cataloging-in-Publication Data
Will, Robin, 1948-
    Beauty of Texas / text, Robin Will: concept & design, Robert D. Shangle / Rev. ed.
      p.   cm.
ISBN 1-55988-315-4; $19.95 — ISBN 1-55988-314-6 (pbk.); $9.95
    1. Texas — Description and travel — 1981 — Views. I. Shangle, Robert D. II. Title.
F387.W63 1992
976.4 — dc20   91-21135
                                                CIP

Contents

Introduction

The writer who approaches an overall view of the State of Texas sets himself a challenging task. The incredible scope and diversity in the geography and people of Texas are forces that work against any reliable generalization. Visitors to Texas are not likely to be able to fathom the depths of history and tradition that make the Lone Star State special, and even lifelong Texans can occasionally find themselves surprised by the variety and contrast their state contains.

Though *generalities* are hard to come by, there is no end to the interesting *particulars* that make up the Texas scene. Texans have a strong sense of identity, a fact that is reassuring when the style and tone of many areas — especially in the cities — seems to be moving in the direction of bland standardization. The terms Ohioan, Pennsylvanian or Californian may not call a specific image to mind, but if you say "Texan," everybody knows what you're talking about — or thinks they do. There is an aura, a mystique, an ambience that is distinctly and uniquely Texan. Outsiders recognize it, and Texans know it for a fact.

The sense of variety even goes as far as governments. Six flags have flown over Texas during its colorful history. The banners of Spain, France, Mexico, the Republic of Texas, the Confederacy, and the United States have all waved over this sprawling territory. And the multiplicity of governments is duplicated in the state's environments: the semi-arid Trans-Pecos, the rugged Hill Country, the lush Piney Woods, and the spectacular Gulf Coast are difficult to imagine within the same boundaries. The problem comes down to deciding what to mention and what to leave out. Texans have plenty to be proud of, but a complete list is hard to come by.

So while you may hear about cowboys and Indians and the Old Chisolm Trail — the part of Texas that made it into the movies, and the eyes of the world — it's difficult to remember the native attributes that only Texans are likely to be aware of. Pirates, shrimp boats, mountains, fields of roses, and rice paddies are some of these.

To some people Texas may mean the yawning emptiness of the High Plains, the loneliness of the cowboy, a world of far-flung ranches and rippling fields of wheat. It's true — but it's also true that the city of Dallas is now the seventh-largest city in the United States. It is unique among major American cities because it's not on a waterway, and therefore has no seaport.

Old-timers relish the wild and woolly past of places like El Paso, where the rugged Old West may have held on a little too long for comfort — they may fail to remind you how lively things were in the Gulf Coast town of Galveston when pirate Jean Lafitte was "mayor," in the early 1800s. Today, Galveston is a leading commercial and pleasure port, remembering its racy past with the fondness that time can give to the memory of "bad guys," once the danger and nuisance are gone.

While the Old West myth might have Texans enjoying themselves at a hoedown or barbecue — and many do — the truth is that the only thing "typical" about Texas celebrations is the amount of fun you can have at one of them. Galveston's Blessing of the Fleet and the Shrimp Festival; Tyler's Rose Festival; the *Wurstfest* (Sausage Festival) at New Braunfels; Fiesta Week in Old San Antonio; and the World Championship Chili Cook-Off at Terlingua offer a variety of evidence regarding the Texan capacity for *fiesta*.

The subject of non-bovine livestock — sheep and goats, to be precise — is mentioned quietly in Texas, if it is mentioned at all. In the early days, before fences, there were quarrels between sheepmen and cowboys about possession of the range; and even today Texans prefer the image of cattlemen. Although sheep and goats never made it into the movies, the fact is that Texas produces about 97 per cent of all American mohair, and plenty of other wool besides. The scenic Hill Country, not particularly suited to the needs of longhorns, was perfect for other livestock, and the heavily German population of the Hill Country has made wool pay . . . and pay, and pay.

The Germans in the Hill Country are themselves one of the surprises found in Texas. Germans started coming to Texas while it was still a Mexican state, and they filled some counties so completely that through the 1950s some Texan newspapers were still printed in German. The architecture in many Hill Country towns is reminiscent of the Old World, and it's worth a special trip to New Braunfels for the *Wurstfest*, complete with bands, singing societies and other folk traditions that have endured for more than 100 years in the New World.

When Texas joined the Union in 1845, after nine years as a Republic on its own, it retained the right to divide into five separate states, so great was its

8

area. But for the purpose of talking about the state and its scenery, it's easier to utilize a boundary that nature drew, and divide Texas, for the sake of discussion, along the Balcones Escarpment.

Balcones is an ancient slippage plane left from some prehistoric movement of the earth's crust, and it also tends to define some cultural and climatic differences as well. The fault runs from Del Rio on the Rio Grande up through San Antonio and Austin, and on to the Red River and the Oklahoma border. East Texas is the broad, flat remnant of the Greater Mississippi Valley and the Gulf Shelf; West Texas is the southermost extension of the Rocky Mountains and the semi-arid desert. East Texas was once predominantly agricultural, while the west belonged to livestock ranching — though that picture has begun to change. To the south and east of Balcones, rainfall is plentiful. To the west citizens hold prayer meetings for rain and talk about seeding clouds when there are any.

Other meaningful divisions can help make sense of the diversity that is Texas. East of Balcones, on the Texas-Louisiana border, is the region long known as the Piney Woods — headquarters for the substantial Texas lumber industry. Moving westward towards Balcones, the forest gives way to the rich farming country called Blacklands, for its dark, moist earth. South and west of San Antonio, the earth is good but the moisture is scarce — it took irrigation from the Rio Grande to turn this sunny land into a Winter Garden for vegetables, and further south, one of the nation's primary citrus fruit areas. And of course, all of Texas has a claim on the magnificent Gulf Coast.

West Texas can be divided into three parts — four if you count Big Bend National Park separately. The rugged central Hill Country gives way to the high plains on the north and the arid Trans-Pecos, Texas' western spur. Big Bend National Park is situated on the Rio Grande, where it abruptly swings northeast for more than 100 miles. The scenery is of such spectacular beauty, magnitude, and variety that 700,000 acres of it have been set aside as a national park, preserving the harsh, mountainous terrain that once was a hideout for bandits and border rustlers.

Texans know the value of their land, because they've lived close to it and they've tried to tame it. Sometimes the land fights back, but the Texan sense of humor takes it in stride. In the middle of a dust storm on the plains, a rancher notices a prairie dog, "two hundred feet up and trying to dig out." Another describes the grazing range on a Trans-Pecos ranch: ". . . so sparse that a jackrabbit has to graze at a lope to get enough to keep from starving." With admirable nonchalance, residents of the usually peaceful Gulf Coast say that the occasional hurricane "breaks up the monotony of all that perfection." You can go inland to avoid the blow, they tell you, but if you do, you'll miss the excellent fishing and beachcombing that come immediately afterwards. No matter where you find them, Texans just don't seem to let things get them down. That's probably because when the land is good, it's very good. Few places are capable of rewarding effort with such bounty — though the effort is great, the payoff is sufficient.

Certainly one of the payoffs of living in this great land is the great land itself. What some Americans seek out over great distances, at great expense — a feeling of relationship with nature, of belonging to the land — is available to the Texan who will only look around. The great lonely spaces of the prairies, much like the ocean, compel people to "look out a ways," to see beyond themselves. A fragile, semi-desert ecology is bound to do more than sidewalks and skyscrapers to reaffirm man's delicate ties with the land he lives on. From the hills and bayous of the Piney Woods, to the barren mountains that tower above the Rio Grande; from the oceans of grain in the north, to the surf-pounded shore of the south, the message is clear and it's becoming more relevant all the time: take care of the land and it will take care of you. Texans already have what a great many Americans are looking for: a natural environment that challenges the body, stretches the mind, and refreshes the spirit. It is to the state's never-ending credit that so much that is wild, free and natural has been preserved.

This kind of variety, not to mention the burdens of the state's size, make it a tough job to choose four dozen pictures that do justice to Texas. What's "typically Texan," anyway — the woodlands in the east, the grassland in the west, the cowboy and his herds, or the fleet of shrimp boats on the Gulf of Mexico? When you talk about Texas livestock, do you mean the world-famous beef cattle, or sheep and goats that once touched off range wars? Texas is big enough, in size, scope, and spirit, to take it all in, throw in some oil wells for good measure, and top it off with a shining city or two. Texas can do it all.

All a single book can do with a subject the size of Texas is to offer a hint of the reality of the thing. We can show you more than cowboys, but not as much as there is to show — we hope to offer this book, like a menu, to whet the palate for the portion of Texas that must be experienced to be understood. For that, you have to see for yourself — drive around Texas, and discover the things that aren't on the map: the graciousness and hospitality, the warmth and humor of the place that's the Old West, and so much more.

R.W.

Piney Woods and The Blacklands

A good place to start exploring Texas is the area where the earliest settlers started — the timber belt and farm country of East Texas. South of the Red River and west of the Sabine, defined on the west by the giant stairstep of the Balcones Escarpment, lush farm and timberland rolls down to the sea at Beaumont and Port Arthur. We're considering two geological areas together; the East Texas forests of pine and hardwood shade toward the west into a virtually flat land with waxy, black soil that gives it the name of Blacklands.

This is country with a memory that goes way back. When the American colonies were still 60 years away from independence, there were settlers in Texas, and East Texas has the ruins of two Spanish missions to prove it. Stephen F. Austin's Old Three Hundred settled along the Brazos and Colorado rivers. East Texas sent men to fight Santa Anna at San Jacinto for independence; and many small town monuments commemorate the days when Texas was an independent Republic. Half humorous legends of Confederate conscription gangs hunting down early day draft dodgers in the Big Thicket recall Texas' involvement in another war. And for more recent history, nothing beats the story of Spindletop . . . the area's first oil well, a gusher just outside of Beaumont.

You'll never quite get away from the influence of oil in East Texas, but farmers and loggers had been in the Piney Woods for a long time before the oilmen arrived, and their work goes on. As much of the richness of this area comes from the top of the land as is pumped from underneath it. Cotton is king and has been since the ground was first broken. Though oil derricks are tall, they don't look too big compared to the stands of timber that dominate much of the landscape. The farms that generations of families have carved out of the woods produce a variety of crops: roses and azaleas are grown in commercial quantity in one colorful area, and the rice paddies around Beaumont are among the nation's most productive.

In some ways the recurring cottonfields, rolling hills, piney woods, and red dirt roads conjure up visions of the Deep South. To be sure the similarities are there. But there's something else, as well: a restored Spanish mission, an occasional monument to the Texas Revolution, the bustle and hum of the oil business, and the general energy and scope of a people accustomed to thinking big. The Texan ambience remains foremost.

East Texas is lake and river country. The lakes, mostly man-made for flood control and irrigation, make East Texas a popular area for fishermen, campers, and water sportsmen. Set in the rolling, wooded hills of this region, they provide unequalled scenic opportunities for local residents and visitors from the state's drier areas.

Tyler is in a portion of the rich Blackland country, but unlike the rest of the area, where cotton is grown, in Tyler the production of flowers is the most important industry. Tyler's nurseries supply about half the field grown rose bushes in the United States, and a great many of the azaleas as well. The Texas Rose festival is celebrated in Tyler in early fall — on a scale suitable for the town that's the Rose Capital of the World. Or you can visit in the early spring in time for Azalea Trails and Spring Flower Show, when home gardens are open, and when redbud, dogwood, and wisteria add to the festive event that heralds the coming of spring.

The area around Tyler and Jacksonville is timbered with dense forests of pine and hardwood. Log trucks crowd the road — this is the center of the lumbering industry in Texas. Where land is cleared, small family farms and orchards are commonplace. Down around Rusk, on US Highway 69, turpentine is extracted from long leaf pines in much the same way as maple syrup is taken from maple trees. After refining, both the turpentine and the remaining rosins can be sold.

Around Alto, a small town active in tomato canning and cotton ginning, are some interesting historical remnants that go back as far as the earliest known Texans. State Highway 21 runs south and west of Alto through some of the prettiest scenery around. Six or seven miles out of town is Mound Prairie, a pair of huge ceremonial mounds of the Hasani Indian culture. Unlike some of the other Indian mounds in Texas, which were kitchen middens, these 300 × 350-foot giant knolls had some ceremonial purpose. There's a vaguely eerie feeling as you stand in the quiet countryside, wondering about the people who built these earthworks and the uses they were put to.

There is more recent history nearby; the Weches Alto area was the site of early Spanish missionary activity to the Indians. Near the Indian mounds is the site of the re-establishment of the Mission of San Francisco de los Tejas. The mission was maintained in these parts from 1716 to 1719, given up, and

12

re-established in 1721. Further down the road at Weches is the original site of the mission at Mission San Francisco de los Tejas State Historic Park. A replica of the mission is one of several early day structures in the park.

Stay on State Highway 21 through the Davy Crockett National Forest for a glimpse of the way this country must have looked in the days before settlement. The dim, fragrant forest shelters ponds and bayous that offer excellent fishing for perch and catfish. The unusual road signs warning you to WATCH OUT FOR HOGS prompt the inevitable road hog jokes, but they'd best be taken seriously. They refer to razorbacks, wild descendants of the hogs brought in more than two centuries ago by Spanish explorers. They're known hereabouts as "piney rooters." Nothing much scares them and their reputation for viciousness is established beyond a doubt. Anyone can claim an unmarked wild hog by putting his mark on the critter's ear . . . after he catches it.

East of Alto, in the area around Douglass, is country that preserves some mementoes of the Texas Revolution. Mission buffs, as well, will find delight in visiting the sites of several old missions. Some are easily accessible, while others require that you check locally for word about road conditions. On the old San Antonio-Nacogdoches road is the site of Mission Nuestra Senora de la Purisima Conception (Mission of Our Lady of the Immaculate Conception) established in 1716 and abandoned in 1730. Another mission that spanned exactly the same years operated a few dozen miles away outside of Cushing, on a hill overlooking Bill Creek: Mission San Jose de los Nazonis (Mission St. Joseph of the Nazonis) was also founded in 1716 and given up in 1730.

A drive south and east brings the traveler to the edge of the Big Thicket, a forest that once covered nearly a million acres. Every variety of pine and hardwood native to this latitude can be found here, as well as vines, creepers, shrubs, orchids and so forth that grow in and underneath the trees. The forest is virtually impassible off the beaten tracks. Bears and panthers still roam here and fishing is good.

The difficulty in penetrating the wooded fastness has spawned a variety of legends of lost travelers, sudden disappearances, probable murders, and, of course, ghosts. During the Civil War men anxious to avoid service in the Confederate army hid out here, winning the name "bushwhackers." Conscription details of the Confederacy hunted the fugitives and occasional battles were the result. Other characters who didn't care to be found have drifted in and out of the woods from time to time as well. One thing in the Big Thicket that *does* disappear suddenly is Lost Creek, which drops into a hole at the foot of a big tree and reappears just as suddenly from under a bank of ferns southeast of Saratoga, more than five miles away!

South of the Big Thicket, lumbering country gives way to the vivid colors and flat land of rice paddies. Jefferson County alone devotes thousands of acres to rice culture, and rice was Beaumont's main commodity in the years before the discovery of oil. The low prairies of the east coastal plain were ideal for growing rice because the lands were easy to flood. Rice paddies, of coures, mean fences, and the original rice growers were held in low esteem by fence-hating cattlemen whose fortunes depended on open range and unlimited grazing. Today, the brilliant green rice fields stretch for miles across coastal prairies, and few cities in the United States ship as much rice as Beaumont.

The Blacklands, the strip of land directly to the west of the Piney Woods, is harder to define but well worth the attention. The Blacklands contains the cities of Fort Worth, Dallas, Waco, Austin, and San Antonio — and, as any Texan knows, the towns aren't the half of it. This is some of the best farmland in Texas or anywhere else. The traveler who puts his mind to it can steer around the big cities and spend his time in the rich valleys of the Trinity, Brazos and Colorado rivers.

In the north the town of Gainesville occupies the center of the Blackland belt. The land is rich, rolling prairie, given over to a variety of agricultural uses; enormous harvests of wheat, grain, and cotton find their way into Gainesville, as do livestock and poultry. The town occupies the broad valley of the Elm Fork of the Trinity: it's a shady town with brick-paved streets that pass many homes from the 19th century. Flower gardens are a matter of local pride. Outside of town to the northwest is Moss Lake, Gainesville's water supply and a good place to do some fishing.

Over towards Sherman and Denison, spectacular Lake Texoma draws its share of visitors. Impoundment of the Red River created a lake covering more than 89,000 acres — the shoreline is 580 miles long, shared wth Oklahoma. Fishing is good for black bass, crappie, catfish, and the like, and there's room for every variety of boating activity. On the Big Mineral arm of Texoma is Hagerman National Wildlife Refuge, offering food and shelter for migratory waterfowl on a grassy plain adjoining the lake.

South of Denton US Highway 77 parallels the Trinity River, a country of lush and heavily wooded bottomlands. This area produces a variety of fruits and berries as well as the ubiquitous cotton, and in season roadside stands sell fruit and cider. There's good fishing practically everywhere.

South of Dallas the land is drained by a series of picturesque rivers that make their way to the Gulf Coast. This area was settled originally by southern planters, and it was early established as a cotton-producing empire stretching

14

for miles on each side of the Brazos. The plantation economy never really worked in Texas, and, today, the broad plain south of Dallas, and the rougher lands of the Trinity and Brazos watersheds, are frequently family operated.

South of Waco are a couple of towns that enjoy the unusual amenity of piped-in hot water. In the mid-twenties, a man drilling for oil in Chilton struck a resource he wasn't looking for: hot water. Enterprising citizens put it to good use in their homes. In nearby Marlin an artesian hot-water well was considered useless for years until stories began to circulate of miraculous cures effected by bathing in the run-off ditch. Today, the hot-water resource is used in spas, hospitals, and clinics for its curative powers.

The fertile Blacklands continue as far south as San Antonio and somewhat beyond, squeezed up against the Balcones Escarpment and the higher, drier Hill Country on the north. Balcones, itself, provides some scenery on the northern edge of the Blacklands. As a line of massive slippage in the earth's crust, the escarpment exposes some interesting geological strata, one cavern, and a river. The San Marcos River emerges where huge springs pour about 98 million gallons of clean, cold water per day from the foot of a cliff.

San Marcos is the home of two world-stature contests. One is a canoe race from San Marcos to the sea. Beginning at Aquarena Springs, contestants must carry all the supplies required to traverse hundreds of miles of river and saltwater. The race ends at Seadrift on the Gulf Coast. The other contest is also of prime importance to Texas and the world: the Republic of Texas Chilympiad is held here. It's a state chili-cooking contest, held to choose a champion to represent Texas at the World Chili Cook-Off (also held in Texas at Terlingua). Just because Texans have a lot of fun at this event is no indication that they're not taking it seriously: chili is an important matter in Texas. It's worth a trip to San Marcos in September for this good-time event. The true chili fanciers will make it over to Big Bend country to Terlingua for the World Championship and assorted hi-jinks later in the fall.

For those who enjoy their scenery on the cool and dark side, the Balcones Escarpment has provided Wonder Cave, a cavern created by earthquake and erosion, 150 feet below the earth's surface. It's within the city limits of San Marcos.

San Antonio is the last city of any size to reap the wealth of the Blacklands. At this point the region becomes known by other names, and the amount of moisture in the environment declines noticeably. The land to the south and west of San Antonio is where the great Texas cattle industry had its beginnings. But that's another story.

South Texas and The Gulf Coast

South of San Antonio, Texas descends on a rolling plain to the ocean, the sun-drenched Gulf Coast. In the east the country is well-watered and rich, yielding its abundance in farm and pastureland. South and west of San Antonio, the land is just as rich, but not as wet. Irrigation in the last 50-plus years has produced a remarkable change in certain sections that once could support only cattle. The result is that a person can stand in Brownsville, on the Rio Grande, and see sights that haven't changed noticeably since the days of the Republic — and then turn around to face green and fragrant citrus groves that stretch almost out of sight, where once was only mesquite.

The coastal plain and the dry southlands played an important part in Texas history, and the area has seen people of many nationalities try to stake claims on its rich shores. LaSalle, the French explorer, was murdered by his own men on a trip of exploration in 1687. Spaniards, worried about French incursions in the area, established Mission Nuestra Senora del Refugio in 1790, and the town, its name mercifully shortened to Refugio, exists today. The beginnings of the Texas cattle economy came from the south of Texas as well. Yoakum, which, today, holds a harvest festival devoted to tomatoes, once resounded with the cries of men and horses moving enormous herds of cattle to market. The great King Ranch, the nation's biggest and best-known, lies in this area.

There are even two interesting and romantic bad-guys in the history of the southern edge of Texas. After the War of 1812, French-American pirate Jean Lafitte, who had worn out his welcome in Louisiana, spent a few years enlivening Galveston and its environs. Lafitte renamed the island settlement Campeachy, and contructed a home/warehouse/fortress from which he terrorized Spanish shipping, taking nearly 100 ships in three years. The Spaniards, spread thin in the Western hemisphere, were powerless in the face of this villainy. Any appeal they made to the United States to make Lafitte desist would have been recognition that Americans, rather than Spanish, held

The Alamo, San Antonio

Santa Elena Canyon, Rio Grande River

Bluebonnets in Texas Hill Country

Guadalupe Peak

Near Burnham

Castle Gap

El Capitan

Palo Duro

Near Independence

Sawtooth Mountains near Fort Davis

Padre Island

Ocotillo

Presidio La Bahia

Hamilton Pool

Near Daingerfield

Cypress Creek

West Texas' Pecos River

Mission San Jose

West of Groesbeck

Lower Rio Grande area

Sunset near Amarillo

Yucca near Marathon

Horsecollar Bluff north of Leaky

Near Hempstead

Near Gainesville, Texas

Caddo Lake

Mason County

Near the Pecos River in West Texas

Near Medina

Near Lamesa

Southern Methodist University, Dallas

Davis Mountains

Dallas

State Capitol Building, Austin

Mason County

Corpus Cristi

Houston

Point Isabel Lighthouse

Fort Worth

Guadalupe River

San Antonio

Mission at Goliad

Rio Grande River near Langtry

Rio Grande River

Oil Drill Rig at Sunset near Weslaco

Pedernales River near LBJ Ranch, Stonewall

Near Canyon Lake in Central Texas Hill Country north of New Braunfels

Pecos River

authority in Texas. A rowdy and bawdy little town, full of adventurers from all points of the compass, grew up around Lafitte's fortress, with a pair of French generals and some 400 gentlemen adventurers adding a continental touch. Things went well until Lafitte's men began taking American ships — an outcry went up in the United States to clean out the pirate's nest, but before the Americans could move, a hurricane did most of the job for them. Lafitte, under heavy American pressure, cleared out the following May, leaving the town in flames.

In the west, about fifty years later, a Mexican Robin Hood named Juan Nepomuceno Cortinas rose from the ranks of Mexican ranchers to protest abuses of land rights in the Brownsville area. Non-Latin Texans were confiscating lands on the north side of the Rio Grande, which Mexicans held under old Spanish grants. American courts were in no mood to recognize the authority of Spanish grants. Vowing to fight with force if necessary, Cortinas rode into Brownsville with about 100 followers on September 28, 1859. They killed five men who offered resistance, sacked stores, turned prisoners out of jail, and threatened to burn the town. Finally, the Mexican government persuaded Cortinas to ride back to his headquarters at Santa Rita.

But Cortinas had found a large and sympathetic following, and worried citizens of Brownsville mounted an expedition to put an end to this threat. The battle was over almost before it began: Brownsville forces retreated with such haste that they left their cannons behind. Texas Rangers were also unable to whip Cortinas in his Santa Rita stronghold, and two months later, United States troops marched against Santa Rita, driving Cortinas back into Mexico. From that relative safety, he continued to raid towns and ranches north of the Rio Grande until joint action by the Mexican and American governments put an end to the harassment.

But bad guys are mostly interesting in the past tense, as they're either disturbing or dangerous to live with, and they tend to slow down the work of the real heroes of a frontier. They are the ordinary folk who move into a new region and endure hardship and privation while wresting their living from the earth. The bad guys made their mark in history — the rest made their marks on the land.

South and west of San Antonio the country is low and flat. Where it has not been cleared, it is covered with sagebrush and mesquite. As you move into the Winter Garden, where land is cleared and irrigated, the country is checkerboarded with fields and citrus groves. Around Crystal City spinach is the big cash crop, and when Crystal City calls itself the Spinach Capital of the World, no one argues. Truck farmers in this area harvest four vegetable crops a year. Enthusiasm for the local specialty went so far that in 1937 the city erected a statue of Popeye, the belligerent, spinach-eating sailor, in the town square.

Away from cultivation and irrigation, the chapparal jungles begin. There's a local saying that everything in the chapparal either bites, stings, or sticks. Panthers, wild hogs, coyotes, and wildcats can be found if you're looking for them; deer, dove and quail hunting are also excellent. Beware of rattlesnakes, and take the local tall tales about snake charming with a note of skepticism. Nobody's going to say they're not true, but rattlesnake charming is a pastime best left to the experienced.

Southward, through the Winter Garden town of Carrizo Springs, date palms bear heavily. Some of the cattle ranches in this area exceed 100,000 acres and extend to the Rio Grande. Where the land is irrigated, crops include onions, carrots, cabbage, cauliflower, cucumbers, cantaloupes, and the like. You leave the Winter Garden in Catarina, a town with a great many palm trees and relatively few people, and move south into brush-covered rangelands.

South of Laredo, US Highway 83 roughly parallels the Rio Grande through barren, semi-arid plains to the rolling sagebrush around Zapata. By that time the sight of water is welcome, and there's plenty of water in Lake Falcon, a reservoir nearly 40 miles long, created by a dam on the Rio Grande at Falcon Heights. The waters of the lake, shared with Mexico, define a shoreline more than 375 miles in length. US Highway 83 follows the bank of the lake through hills covered with purple sage, which gradually flatten out to become the Rio Grande Valley.

Actually not a valley at all, the broad, irrigated farmlands at the southern tip of Texas really make up the delta of the Rio Grande. Seventy-five years ago it was scrubby wilderness, producing cotton where the land was cultivated. Today it is one of the world's leading citrus districts, the result of irrigation and lots of hard work. Shiny dark-green date palms line the roads and form windbreaks for the lighter-green citrus groves; bamboo and wild cane grow along irrigation canals, and almost every house has its brilliant bougainvillea vine. Winter brings out poinsettias that grow wild beside the roads. There's almost always a harvest in process here. Winter produces an extravaganza of oranges and famous Texas Ruby grapefruit, while in summer, tons of cotton, sugar cane and grain. During other seasons, vegetables such as peas, lettuce, carrots, spinach or cabbage are abundant.

From Brownsville there's nowhere in Texas to go except north, and it's a good place to begin exploring the Gulf Coast. Access to Padre Island National

Seashore is at Port Isabel: the 110-mile island has largely been left undisturbed by man. Although furnished with roads along much of its length, most people stay in the developed areas at either end of the island, Port Isabel and at Nueces County Park and Padre Island National Seashore near Corpus Christi.

In between is an 80-mile stretch of narrow, sandy island generally in its natural state. Constantly shifting sands occasionally uncover wrecks of ancient ships, but more frequently they cover everything with smooth, windblown dunes up to 30 feet high. Sun, surf, and primitive beach camping are the main attractions of the ocean side of the island, while the sheltered waters between the leeward coast and the mainland offer a rich estuarine environment to fish and waterfowl. Through-traffic along the length of the island is mercifully prevented by the Port Mansfield Cut, an artificial channel that divides the island. People who appreciate palm-fringed resort areas tend to stay at the ends of the island, leaving the middle for those who are prepared for sunny and primitive solitude.

The motorists who get on Padre Island at Port Isabel get off there, too, since the causeway is the only access to the south island. The way north is on US Highway 77, traveling the flat coastal plain several miles inland on the way to the port city of Corpus Christi. On the way the road goes through Kingsville, headquarters of the famous King Ranch. It's the largest ranch in the continental United States, down somewhat from more than a million acres to a mere 823,000. Captain King, a Rio Grande steamboat captain, began acquiring land in 1853 with the purchase of Santa Gertrudis, a Spanish land grant, and he never stopped. The enormous ranch is still run by descendants of one of Captain King's daughters. Once based on the Texas Longhorn, today King Ranch leads in producing purebred cattle, including the Santa Gertrudis strain, which was developed here. It's possible to take a 12-mile drive around the ranch, though the complexity of business makes it impossible for the ranch to provide tours or accept casual visitors.

Some of the best of the coastline can be seen by the traveler who forsakes US 77 at Sinton and turns south on Texas 35 to Aransas Pass, a town where the main business is commercial and sport fishing, and shrimping. From there it's possible to drive up the coast to Rockport. Aside from the seafood, fishing, and recreational opportunities one expects from a coastal town, the Aransas National Wildlife Refuge is nearby. It's the principal wintering ground for the nearly extinct whooping crane, as well as a few hundred other species of birds and animal wildlife. Public access is permitted along designated roads and trails, and a few observation towers provide opportunities to get a look at the rare whoopers, who are here in greatest numbers between November and March.

From Rockport State Highway 35 sneaks across nearly level, occasionally wooded, land into Port Lavaca, which sits on a bluff overlooking Lavaca Bay. This town faces both ways: inland to the ranches and farms and out to sea, where commercial and pleasure fishing bring in visitors and dollars. Port Lavaca is the town that replaced Indianola as county seat after the latter was destroyed by a series of epidemics and disastrous storms. There's a little irony in the statue of La Salle that surveys the site of the old town: the view over the pristine sands, today, must be much the same as the first glimpse La Salle got of this land when he arrived here 300 years ago. Where Indianola was concerned, the intervening years have meant nothing.

North, again, through Palacios and Bay City, a new element appears in the landscape: paddies, flooded and growing brilliant, green shoots of rice, reflect the sun. The petroleum industry is active in Bay City as well, giving the town a multi-faceted economy; petrochemicals, oil, rice, meat, sheet metal, oysters, and shrimp all provide their share of the Bay City payroll. And from Bay City it's not far to the pleasure port of Galveston, once Lafitte's hangout, to the shipping center of Port Arthur and the end of Texas' share of the Gulf Coast.

Hill Country and The Great Plains

The Texas Hill Country lies just to the north of the Balcones Escarpment, that great natural barrier and the 20-inch rainfall line. Geologically and in climate, it has little to do with the broad open spaces of the coastal plains and Blacklands.

Hill Country includes — on its southern/eastern edge — the towns of San Antonio, San Marcos, and Austin. San Marcos sits *right* on the edge, and its river, mentioned elsewhere, flows from springs at the base of Balcones itself. It's typical of many Hill Country streams: cold, artesian water from underground, which probably last saw the sun as snow in the Rocky Mountains, a thousand miles away. The streams don't quite make up for the rainfall differential, however. Hill Country is on the dry side of the 20-inch rainfall line, and residents get the typical Texas sunshine without the humidity of the southlands.

Here is some of Texas' most glorious scenery. This is a mountainous land of granite outcrops, and thin limestone soils cut by springfed streams. Only the narrow valleys have enough soil for farming; the hills are timbered with juniper and cedar, fading into mesquite on the high flatlands of the north, while enormous stands of cypress dominate the valleys. The combination of running water above ground and limestone below has produced some interesting caverns underneath Hill Country, including one so large that it has never been completely explored. Many of the caverns are open for tours of their cool, echoing stillnesses, hung with the fantastic forms of limestone worn away in one place and deposited in another by the dripping waters.

Hill Country is a land of much different character than the Piney Woods or the Gulf Coast, and people of different character were the first settlers there. Neither cotton planters from the old South nor the new breed of Texas cattlemen tamed the Hill Country. The first serious settlements here were by Germans, who recognized good sheep country when they saw it. Though there was some difficulty with Indians, there is a notable absence of bandits, pirates, and other colorful characters: the land was built by thrift and hard work. The names of many of the towns reflect the German heritage: Fredericksburg, New Braunfels, Boerne, Berheim, Luchenbach, and Eckert all carry a slight old-world accent to this day.

New Braunfels was founded by the Society for Protection of German Immigrants in Texas in 1845 and named for its first administrator, Prince Carl Zu Solms-Braunfels. Plagued by hardship and disease, the Society administered the colony until 1853, and then Texas creditors were assigned rights to the community. The frontier proved too much of a challenge for the noblemen, and they returned their homeland. The farmers stayed on, recognizing the opportunity that the land held, and built a rich and close-knit community through their labors. The German influence is still strong in New Braunfels, in some exceedingly pleasant ways. One is the *Wurstfest* (sausage festival) that happens early in November.

New Braunfels has the distinction of having what may be the world's shortest big river within its city limits. The Comal River rises at Comal Springs and flows deep, clear and strong for a total of four miles before it empties into the Guadalupe. Giant caladiums, which grow along its banks, give it a faintly tropical air.

The area around Boerne and New Braunfels is as remarkable for the scenery underground as for the hills and trees topside. Between Boerne and New Braunfels is Natural Bridge Cavern, a recently-discovered limestone cave that stretches more than a mile under the ranchlands of the Hill Country. Another cavern lies just south of Boerne: Cascade Caverns, known for generations but not fully explored until the 1930s, offers huge crystal pools, sparkling limestone formations that beggar the imagination, and a 90-foot underground waterfall. Still another cavern, Cave Without a Name, lies northeast of town and offers more of the same for the individual who likes his scenery underground.

The country grows more rugged to the north. US Highway 87 penetrates the heart of the Hill Country on its way to San Angelo, climbing hills only to drop into deep green valleys that lie beyond. Hillsides are covered with oak, pecan, cottonwood, and sumac trees, while in the moist valley, stands of cypress keep the scene verdant even in winter. In the autumn colors are superb as the hillsides blaze with frost-tinted leaves, while pinks and greys of granite outcroppings show through the trees or on the faces of cliffs. Whitewater rivers roar through narrow passes, then relax in deep, still streams along the lower valleys.

Stone is the popular building material in this portion of Texas, and some farmhouses give away their age with the loopholes designed to permit rifle fire against Indians and other intruders.

Fredericksburg is another of the Hill Country Germantowns. You're likely to hear German spoken on the streets, enjoy some interesting old-country customs, and partake of the town's famous breads and pastries. A walk around town will provide a chance to see the "Sunday houses," built by early settlers who came to town for Saturday market and Sunday church, then returned to their outlying ranches. Many of these little stone houses survive and are marked by historical medallions, although none are open to the public.

An interesting and poignant tradition is observed here every Easter. More than 100 years ago, an unknown pioneer mother told the story to her children about an Easter rabbit who lit and tended fires on the hillsides to boil eggs for the local children. In reality the fires her youngsters saw belonged to Indians who were camped in the hills awaiting the outcome of peace talks with settlers. The two sides reached agreement and lived in peace in the Pedernales Valley, and today, hillside fires glow each Easter eve while a pageant retells the story.

The area between Fredericksburg and Austin was home base for one of the Hill Country's famous sons, Lyndon Baines Johnson. LBJ State Park is just east of Stonewall, featuring 269 acres with picnic facilities, nature trails, and living wildlife displays: Texas Longhorns, white-tailed deer, and buffalo. A bus tour from park headquarters includes the President's birthplace, his grave, and the nearby LBJ Ranch. The Johnson Boyhood Home in Johnson City is also preserved as a National Historic Site.

About 20 miles north of Fredericksburg is Enchanted Rock, a massive, solid-granite dome with an eerie history that stretches back into the distant past of Indian legends. Once the site of human sacrifice, the dome was sometimes avoided, somtimes used as a rallying point, but never treated with indifference. Indians believed that phantom fires burned there on moonlit nights; geologists believe that the creaking, groaning sounds that come from the rock at night are the results of cooling and contraction after a day's sunshine. Cabins are available for people who want to spend the night and find out for themselves.

The area between Fredericksburg and San Angelo is sheep and goat country for the most part. The landscape remains rugged and is possessed of great variety; livestock graze on the hills and the valleys are farmed. Deer and fowl abound in the oak-covered hills, making this a popular area for hunters from all over Texas.

The advent of fences has somewhat mitigated the early resentment that cattlemen held toward herdsmen of sheep and goats. It's not so much that there were large-scale cattle operations here — the land isn't particularly suited to cattle. But many of the famous cattle trails originating further south came through Hill Country of necessity: the Western Trail went straight through; the Goodnight-Loving Trail started at Fort Belknap on the Brazos and looped south to the Pecos River; and the Chisolm Trail skirted the eastern edge of the region. And it's a fact that sheep and goats crop the grass so close to the ground that cattle cannot graze. Now that herds of cattle are no longer driven overland, that problem no longer exists; and though sheep and goats will never attract the glamour associated with the beef business, Texas is a leading producer of wool and mohair, making the city of San Angelo the largest wool market in the nation.

North of San Angelo, the land smooths out into the High Plains — the yawningly flat country that stretches north as far as Kansas and Nebraska. Once this was open range for the longhorn cattle that made so many Texas fortunes. Indeed, the longhorn, an animal which ". . . could walk 15 miles to water and make one drink last two days," was about the only thing that could live in country where the meager rainfall would not support agriculture. The heritage of the plains is primarily a cowboy heritage.

However, people started poking around underground shortly after the turn of the century and came up with two products that have done a great deal to change the face of this region. In order of discovery, they are oil and water. Oil booms came and went on various parts of the high plains, much as the cattle drives brought flashes of success to prairie outposts 40 or 50 years before. Some were short-lived, and some are still going on.

It was a different story in the 1940s when underground water was discovered in sufficient quantities to irrigate cropland. Today cotton, soybeans, grain sorghum, and other crops stretch in rows across the pool-table flatness of the plains, where the land hasn't been given over to oil wells. Crops are planted in strips that follow the contours of the land in an effort to outwit the problems of erosion and the ever-present wind. The planted strips provide a windbreak for the fallow land in between. . . . If whole fields were left fallow, the soil would blow away. The wavy lines of contour planting give the land a crazy-quilt appearance in places.

There are plenty of substantial towns in the high plains, but for local color and a chance to see the Texan heritage at work, it's fun to visit the small ones. Guthrie, the seat of King County, is an example: it's the commercial center for enormous ranches that cover the entire county. With about 250 people, according to 1988 information, Guthrie claims 25 per cent of the county's population, the rest being spread out over 944 square miles. The oil fields in the eastern part of the county contribute to the area's income, but not much to the population.

Dickens, seat of adjacent Dickens County, commands a population of nearly 300, and again, is the retail center for a large ranching area. Nearby Croton Breaks is a region of colorful canyons, buttes, and small creeks that add interest to the predominantly flat look of things.

Further west are the cities of Midland and Odessa. Beginning with a siding from the Texas and Pacific Railway, the two towns remained small until oil was discovered in 1923. Today the combined population is over 200,000. Sitting in the middle of an immense, dry plain, the two towns are sometimes hit by furious dust and wind storms. Sand dunes outside of town indicate this area was once ocean bottom. Lawns and gardens of the towns add a surprising patch of green to the wide open plains.

The Texas Panhandle offers yet another kind of flat country: dry, flat country. Groundwater resources are limited, so there's not much irrigation. Despite a rainfall that averages significantly less than 20 inches a year, winter wheat makes a good cash crop in this country, so flat that 90 per cent of it can be cultivated. Because of the dry climate, half the land stands fallow each year, gathering water for the next; while on the other half, wheat is planted in September or October to take advantage of winter rains and is harvested in June. Amarillo is the main city of the Panhandle.

The far-flung wheatfields attract attention because of their visibility, but they're not the only thing happening in the Panhandle. Sizeable oil and natural gas operations occur here, and Amarillo is a leader in the production of helium. Helium is a lighter-than-air gas with properties that give it a variety of scientific uses, and it is a bonus that's found in some natural gas deposits.

Outside of Amarillo, in contrast to the flatness, is Palo Duro Canyon, a deep gash cut through the plains by a branch of the Red River. Steep walls plunge almost a thousand feet to the floor of the canyon, and incredible spires, pinnacles, and colonnades stand as evidence of the erosive power of the river. Richly colored layers of stone, exposed by the water's cutting power, are brought to life by the slanting rays of the sun in early morning and late afternoon. Within the park is a historical marker commemorating the last great Indian battle in Texas history.

North of Amarillo, Lake Meredith spreads among the colorful buttes and hills of the Canadian River Valley. Fishermen take walleye, bass, crappie, and catfish from the sparkling blue waters; campers and hikers go up just to enjoy the bare cliffs and hills that roll down to the water's edge.

Trans-Pecos and Big Bend

West of the Pecos River lies the Texas you'll recognize from the movies. It's the wild and woolly frontier, peopled with cowboys, Indians, and outlaws, made exciting by blazing gunfights, lost gold mines, and the stark and dusty landscapes of the Old West. This is land of jagged brown mountains, flat-topped mesas and dry river beds: a place where locals may tell you that each steer needs 150 acres of pasture to survive. Ghost towns, well-preserved in the clear, dry air, tend to underline the fact that in the old days, it was an act of bravery and optimism just to settle here.

This land was the home of Judge Roy Bean, the "Law West of the Pecos," who dispensed a semblance of law and six-shooter justice from his saloon in Langtry. Bean's colorful humor and unorthodox style have made him legendary in Texas; and whatever today's citizens might think of his high-handed, frequently prejudiced rulings, it was clear that it was a marked improvement on what had gone before.

Today things west of the Pecos are not quite so tough. It doesn't rain any more than it ever did, but the severities of climate are softened by discovery of abundant groundwater and the development of irrigation projects in some locations. Oil — a crop that requires no water — provides a significant boost. Cattle are still raised on the range, but nowadays they're likely to be finished in El Paso feedlots on locally-grown grain. Pancho Villa, John Wesley Hardin and the rest of the outlaws live only in memory, the latter having been gunned down in an El Paso street in 1895.

Depending on where you're coming from, you're likely to enter this region either on Highway I-20 or US Highway 90. Interstate 20, the main east-west artery for Texas motorists, lies along the southern edge of the High Plains on the way to Trans-Pecos country. Across the Pecos River, the route is uphill through dusty sagebrush lands, with the Apache Mountains on the right and the wooded Davis Mountains on the left. Average rainfall here is about 12 inches annually, which qualifies this country for the label of semi-desert. The town of Pecos, once and still a cowtown, has been enriched by the Red Bluff Irrigation Project in the north. Today the countryside roundabout produces long-staple cotton, cantaloupes, and feed grains, and oil.

If there's a choice, it's more scenic to enter Trans-Pecos from the south, along the Rio Grande from Del Rio. That way, some river scenery relieves the dry ruggedness of the region. US Highway 90 winds up through barren hills, crossing canyons of two rivers that empty into the Rio Grande. Devil's River Canyon is one, and Castle Canyon, named for its weirdly eroded colonnades high above the river, is the other. Amistad Lake, a joint Mexican-American project for irrigation and flood control, backs up both the Rio Grande and the Devil's river. Further upstream Seminole Canyon's caves once sheltered a prehistoric culture of basket-making people known as West Texas Cave Dwellers, who lived in this area for centuries. Leaving the river at Langtry, home of the aforementioned Judge Roy Bean, the highway sprints across high and rugged lands, where the sage-and-greasewood dotted plains are grazed mostly by sheep and goats.

At Marathon is the gateway to Big Bend National Park (more about that, later). Alpine, a little further down the road, is home town for a number of ranches of particular vastness. Trees line the streets of Alpine, and the town maintains a definitely western style. Where the streets end, the desert begins. West of Alpine the highway winds through Paisano Pass, then drops through mountainous plateau country, barren of vegetation, into the town of Van Horn.

From Van Horn most travelers will go directly into the fertile Rio Grande Valley toward the town of El Paso, granddaddy of all the western towns. After years as a dry and dusty border town, in 1917 it was discovered that El Paso was located above a huge underground lake, and deep wells were sunk to provide an abundance of water for irrigation. The rugged trans-Pecos mountains, clad in the misty purple haze of desert vegetation, now unexpectedly open up to the gardens and farms of the irrigated valley region. Alfalfa, orchards, melons, roses, cottonfields, and vineyards all grow in lush profusion along the irrigation ditches that make them possible. Once a shoot-'em-up cowboy town, El Paso's slogan, today, involves the five Cs — Copper, Cotton, Cattle, Clothing, and Climate.

As recently as 1912, El Paso was swept into the turbulence of Mexican politics when changes in the government made El Paso headquarters for revolutionary juntas. Soldiers of fortune flocked to the border town to take part in the fighting . . . and not all the fighting took place in Mexico. Mobilization of the National Guard regiments turned the Texas side of the Rio Grande into a huge armed camp, and Pancho Villa's raid into New Mexico in 1916 led to Pershing's punitive expedition into Mexico, with the two forces playing tag through the Big Bend country.

Most travelers come to Southwest Texas to see Big Bend National Park, a scenic extravaganza of some 700,000 acres that was set aside in the 1940s to preserve its spectacular natural beauty for posterity. One enters the park into constantly deepening solitude and ruggedness, which has been virtually unchanged over the entire history of man. Most of the ranches and villages, established here after the Indians were controlled, have failed to amount to much against the rigors of climate and isolation, although there are still immense ranches in Brewster County outside the park's limits. Generally, the Big Bend country has remained wild, defying mankind's efforts to contain, control, and dominate. Its unconquerable nature certainly adds to its appeal to lovers of the wild and untamed.

As previously mentioned Marathon is the gateway to the Big Bend National Park. One turns south on US Highway 385 and drives south about 80 miles to the park headquarters, in the middle of the enormous northward bend of the Rio Grande from which the park takes its name. Vegetation around Marathon is at a bare minimum, since water, here, is in short supply. Patchy clumps of coarse grass alternate with a scrubby sage and other desert plants, not quite covering the basin floor and the sharp, rugged peaks that rise into the blue hazes of the distance.

US Highway 385 proceeds directly south into the teeth of the Santiago Range, part of the backbone of the Rockies, which is called Sierra Del Carmen on the Mexican side. Santiago Peak is the greatest of these, and Apache artifacts are still found in an old campsite on the flat top of the peak (6,521 feet), where Indians kept a lookout in the old days. At the last minute, the highway snakes through the all-but-invisible Persimmon Gap, the northernmost gate of the park. The Gap was part of the famous or infamous, Comanche Trail, blazed by raiding Indians from the South Plains on their way to Mexico. The gap is named for the wild persimmon that grows in profusion, hereabouts.

From Persimmon Gap there is an excellent view of the next mountain range, also part of the Rocky Mountain system. High and hazy, the Chisos Mountains stand in the curve of the Rio Grande. Some say the name Chisos comes from an Apache word meaning ghostly, because of the shimmering haze that usually surrounds them. Another possible derivation is from the Comanche word for echo. Either way, the mountains are known for their brilliant colorings from mineral deposits, and for their extreme ruggedness. To the right are the Rosillos Mountains, and behind them loom the Christmas Mountains and the Corazones Peaks in the dim distances.

The road pushes in a southerly direction across Bone Spring Flats, through an area of interest to archaeologists and ancient history buffs. Bone Springs was once a marsh or seep where great numbers of animals bogged down and died, leaving nothing but bleached bones. Further along at Tornillo Creek is a Fossil Bone exhibit, detailing research about the reptiles and mammals that lived here when the land was younger. The road ultimately reaches the Park Headquarters, and the visitor must reach a decision at this point, since the road forks.

Generally speaking, the National Park consists of the land contained in an enormous loop in the Rio Grande. There are dramatic canyons at either end of the loop (accessible by car) and one in the middle (inaccessible except by pack train). Contained in the curve of the river are the Chisos Mountains, encircled to the north by the park road. The Chihuahuan Desert, which makes up most of the park, contains some of the most colorful and vivid desert and badland formations anywhere, while at higher elevations the cool woodlands of the Chisos make an inviting contrast. Along the river where canyon walls permit, the Rio Grande's jungle-like flood plain amply demonstrates what the land can do when it is watered. South, east, or west lies land of unabated magnificence. The only problem is trying to see it all.

Oddly, as harsh as the desert environment may seem, it is quite fragile. Abused and overgrazed for several hundred years, the lands within the Big Bend boundaries are slowly returning to the high-desert range that existed here before the coming of the Spanish. No soothing rains and lush growth appear within short seasons to mask the scars mankind leaves on the land, and a cactus all of six inches tall may have required fifty years to reach that size. Even tire tracks in the desert may last for years, and plants which struggle for mere survival may not be able to rally the strength to repair themselves if damaged by human thoughtlessness. The envirnomental record at Big Bend is good, an encouraging indication that people can learn to make use of these wild, open and free places, without using them up.

The westernmost canyon is the Santa Elena, a spectacular gash through sheet rock, at the bottom of which flows the generally peaceful river, fringed by what greenery can find foothold at the base of the towering walls. It's hard to imagine the peaceful, silted waters were capable of the work they did here, but the river, after a heavy rain upstream, is another animal indeed, wild and rampaging.

The middle canyon is Marsical. No road leads in, so folks who want to visit Marsical Canyon go in with a pack train and camp there.

At the other end of the park is Boquillas Canyon. Its name is Spanish for "little mouth," because of the narrowness of the opening through which the river passes. In this 25-mile gorge, the depth of the canyon averages 1,600 feet, keeping shadows deep except at midday.

The middle of the park is home for the Chisos Mountains, and the campgrounds of The Basin offer a good place to begin exploring the hundreds of miles of trails that penetrate these silent reaches. A road climbs to Green Gulch up a steep grade through pinyons, oaks, and juniper, skirting bare and rugged peaks. From Panther Pass it drops into the Chisos Basin, a huge bowl at the foot of Casa Grande mountain. Accommodations make this an ideal home base for an exploration of the area. As everywhere in the desert, explorers are urged to carry sufficient water, to remain on the trails, and to carry a flashlight at night to avoid surprise meetings with rattlesnakes.

So long, You will,
I'm sorry you have to go.
Don't forget—Happy trails to you.
Hope to see you in Las Vegas. Mountain Rd
my address there is: 7626 W Lone Mountain Rd
Las Vegas, NV 89129
Telephone 702-395-6785
I'll be at Kathy's until June 17th
Be careful and drive carefully,
Marylou DiPollino

Kelly,
I'm sorry that I didn't get to work with you, more then I did. You're interesting and extremely entertaining. I'm not going to tell you that you're a good nurse. because you know that you are! I wish you success and happiness. "Mr Right" will be there when you least expect it, trust me I know.
                    Take care...
                    Barbara